THE ELEMENTS

Tungsten

Kerry Turrell

BENCHMARK BOOKS

MARSHALL CAVENDISH

NEW YORK

Benchmark Books
Marshall Cavendish
99 White Plains Road
Tarrytown, New York 10591

www.marshallcavendish.com

Library of Congress Cataloging-in-Publication Data

Turrell, Kerry.
Tungsten / by Kerry Turrell.
p.   cm. — (The elements)
Includes index.
Summary: Examines the characteristics, sources, and uses of the element tungsten,
as well as tungsten's importance in our lives.
Contents: What is tungsten? — Special characteristics —
Discovery of tungsten — Where tungsten is found —
Mining tungsten ores — Processing the ore —
Tungsten's uses and compounds — Tungsten alloys —
Tungsten carbide — Periodic table — Chemical reactions.
ISBN 0-7614-1548-3
1. Tungsten—Juvenile literature. [1. Tungsten.] I. Title. II.
Elements (Benchmark Books)
QD181.W1T87 2003
546'.536—dc22   2003052099

Printed in China

Picture credits
Front Cover: Andrew Brookes/Corbis
Back Cover: Avocet Mining plc

Avocet Mining plc: 12
Bosch: 26
C. & H. S. Pellant: 10
Callaway Golf Europe Ltd.: 24 (*center*)
Corbis: Jacques Langevin 27
Fotoshots: D. Smith 14
Ingram Publishing: *iii*, 24 (*bottom*)
NASA: 4, 22, 23
National Element Inc.: 19
North American Tungsten Corporation Ltd.: 13 (*top*), 13 (*center*), 13 (*bottom*), 15
Oak Ridge National Laboratory: 25
Science & Society Picture Library: NMPFT 21, Science Museum 6, 18
Science Photo Library: Bruce Frisch 30, Manfred Kage 7, Peter Ryan 11, Andrew Syred *i*, 16
H. C. Starck: 20 (left), 20 (*right*)
Thermal Technologies Inc.: 17 (*left*), 17 (*right*)
University of Pennsylvania Library: 8

Series created by The Brown Reference Group plc
Designed by Sarah Williams
www.brownreference.com

Contents

What is tungsten?

Pure tungsten is a very strong, shiny, gray-white metal that makes up just a tiny fraction of Earth's crust—about $\frac{1}{20}$ ounce (1.5 grams) per ton of rock. Tungsten never occurs as a pure metal in nature. It is always found combined with other elements as compounds.

Today, tungsten and its compounds have many important uses. The high melting point of tungsten makes it the ideal choice for filaments in light bulbs and other heating elements. The metal is also added to steel to make hard, strong, temperature-resistant alloys. Mixed with

Spacecraft can be powered using heat energy from the sun. A hole in a tungsten shield allows sunlight to heat up a tank of gas. The hole then closes and the gas cools. Repeating the cycle powers the engine.

carbon, tungsten forms hard compounds called carbides. These are used to make cutting tools and the tips of drill bits.

The tungsten atom

Everything around you consists of tiny particles called atoms. Atoms are the building blocks of all elements. They are too small to be seen by the naked eye.

Atoms are made up of even smaller particles called protons, neutrons, and electrons. The protons and neutrons cluster together in the dense nucleus at the center of each atom. The electrons revolve around the nucleus in layers called electron shells.

Every tungsten atom has 74 positively charged protons in the nucleus. No other element shares this number, so tungsten has an atomic number of 74. The number of protons and electrons is the same, so there are 74 negatively charged electrons revolving around the nucleus. Electrons balance the positive charge of the protons, making the atom electrically neutral.

TUNGSTEN ATOM

Nucleus

First shell
Second shell
Third shell
Fourth shell
Fifth shell
Sixth shell

The number of protons in the nucleus of an atom matches the number of electrons revolving around the nucleus. Each tungsten atom has 74 protons in its nucleus and 74 electrons revolving around the nucleus. The electrons revolve in 6 layers called electron shells. There are 2 electrons in the inner shell, 8 in the second shell, 18 in the third shell, 32 in the fourth shell, 12 in the fifth shell, and 2 in the outer shell.

Neutrons are about the same size as protons, but they have no electrical charge. Tungsten has different versions of its atoms, called isotopes, that contain different numbers of neutrons. Some isotopes are radioactive, which means they break down into other elements. The isotopes of tungsten that contain 108 and 110 neutrons are called stable isotopes, because they are not radioactive. There are three other stable isotopes of tungsten, with 106, 109, and 112 neutrons.

Tungsten powder adds strength and hardness to this diamond-tipped steel drill bit. This drill bit is used to drill through rock to find oil or gas.

DID YOU KNOW?

ATOMIC MASS

The atomic mass of an element is given by the number of neutrons and protons in its atoms. Tungsten has five stable isotopes. The number of protons is the same for each isotope, but the number of neutrons is different. To find the atomic mass of tungsten, you have to calculate the average number of neutrons for all five isotopes. Adding 106, 108, 109, 110, and 112, and then dividing by 5, equals 109. So there is an average of 109 neutrons in a tungsten atom. The atomic mass of tungsten is the average number of neutrons (109) plus the number of protons (74). This equals 183. You can check the atomic numbers of tungsten and all the other elements in the periodic table on pages 28 and 29.

Forming compounds

Tungsten's electrons occupy six electron shells. The first four shells are full, but the fifth and sixth shells are incomplete. The behavior of the outer electrons determines how tungsten combines with other elements to form compounds. When tungsten reacts with other elements it tries to share or exchange the electrons in the last two electron shells. When a tungsten atom donates electrons to other elements, it then has a positive charge and is called an ion.

Special characteristics

Tungsten is a very dense metal with a dull, gray appearance. One cubic inch of tungsten weighs nearly twice as much as one cubic inch of lead. Tungsten is also fairly brittle—you could cut a piece with a hacksaw. Despite this, tungsten is one of the strongest of all the metals. Tungsten displays most of its amazing properties at very high temperatures.

Tungsten has the highest melting point of all the elements except carbon. It starts to melt (turn to liquid) when metals such as iron have already reached their boiling point. At high temperatures, tungsten keeps its strength and does not expand as much as other metals.

A false-color scanning electron micrograph (SEM) reveals crystals of pure tungsten.

TUNGSTEN FACTS	
Chemical symbol:	W
Atomic number:	74
Melting point:	6,152 °F (3,410 °C)
Boiling point:	10,220 °F (5,660 °C)
Density:	11.1 ounces per cubic inch (19.25 g/cm^3)
Isotopes:	Five natural isotopes (around twenty-one artificial isotopes)
Name's origin:	The word *tungsten* comes from the Swedish words *tung* and *sten,* meaning "heavy stone"

Chemical properties

Tungsten does not react with many other substances. It resists attack by most acids, although it will dissolve in a mixture of highly concentrated nitric acid (HNO_3) and hydrofluoric acid (HF). However, tungsten readily forms strong alloys with other metals such as chromium and iron.

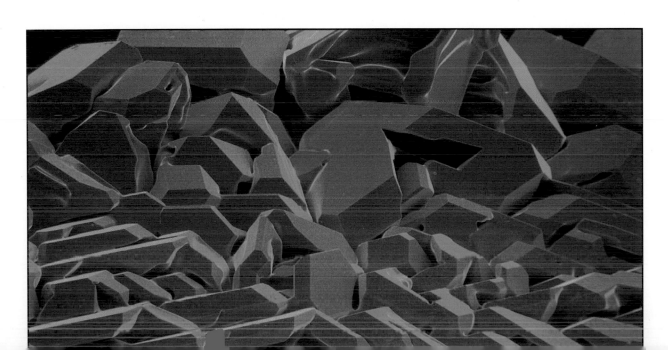

Discovery of tungsten

Tin miners in Germany were the first people to notice the effects of a tungsten compound in the sixteenth century. The miners came across a mineral that interfered with the reduction of cassiterite, a tin mineral. (Reduction removes oxygen from a mineral, leaving the pure metal, in this case, tin.) A miner wrote: "They [the minerals] tear away the tin and devour it like a wolf devours a sheep." The miners gave the mineral the German name *Wolfrahm,* which means "wolf froth." They did not realize that they had witnessed the effects of a new element.

A portrait of Spanish chemist Fausto d'Elhuyar y de Suvisa who, aided by his brother Juan José, isolated pure tungsten in 1783.

Heavy stone

In 1755, Swedish chemist and mineralogist Axel Frederik Cronstedt (1722–1765) discovered a particularly dense mineral. He was convinced that it contained an unidentified element. Cronstedt called the mineral *tung-sten*—Swedish for "heavy stone." In 1781, Swedish chemist Carl Wilhelm Scheele (1742–1786) analyzed this mineral and succeeded in isolating lime (calcium carbonate; $CaCO_3$) and an unknown acid he called tungstic acid (H_2WO_4). Scheele and a colleague Torbern Bergman (1735–1784) worked out that tungstic acid contained a new element, but neither chemist could find a

way to purify the metal. Nevertheless, in honor of Scheele's contribution to the early chemistry of tungsten, the mineral *tung-sten* is now called scheelite.

Isolating tungsten

Progress toward isolating tungsten came in 1779, when a chemist named Peter Woulfe (1727–1803) crushed a sample of wolframite and boiled the mineral in hydrochloric acid (HCl). The rich yellow residue that was left led him to believe that the mineral contained a new substance.

Four years later, Woulfe's deduction was proved to be correct. Two of Bergman's students, Spanish chemists Juan José

ATOMS AT WORK

Tungsten metal can be prepared from tungsten trioxide by reduction with powdered carbon. Tungsten trioxide consists of one hydrogen atom attached to three oxygen atoms.

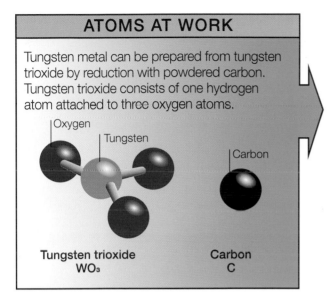

Oxygen
Tungsten
Carbon

Tungsten trioxide
WO_3

Carbon
C

In the first part of the reduction reaction, the carbon atom pulls one of the oxygen atoms from the tungsten trioxide molecule. Tungsten dioxide and carbon monoxide gas form.

Tungsten dioxide
WO_2

Carbon monoxide
CO

The carbon monoxide molecule then pulls off another oxygen atom from the tungsten dioxide molecule. Tungsten oxide and carbon dioxide form.

Tungsten oxide
WO

Carbon dioxide
CO_2

A second carbon atom then pulls off the last oxygen atom from the tungsten oxide to leave tungsten metal and carbon monoxide. But the reaction does not stop there. The resulting carbon monoxide molecule goes off to attack another tungsten trioxide molecule. In this way, more tungsten metal is obtained as the reactions continue.

Tungsten metal
W

Carbon monoxide
CO

The reactions that take place can be written like this:

$$WO_3 + C \rightarrow WO_2 + CO$$
$$WO_2 + CO \rightarrow WO + CO_2$$
$$WO + C \rightarrow W + CO$$

d'Elhuyar y de Suvisa (1754–1804) and his brother Fausto (1755–1833), showed that wolframite contained the same tungstic acid that Scheele had found in scheelite. They prepared tungsten trioxide (WO_3) from crushed wolframite. Then they isolated tungsten from the oxide using carbon as a reducing agent—the substance that removes oxygen from the oxide. This same basic technique, now more than two hundred years old, remains the best way to produce tungsten metal.

An element renamed

The d'Elhuyar y de Suvisa brothers posted news of their discovery to the Academy of Sciences of Toulouse on March 4, 1784. They called the metal wolfram, after the mineral wolframite. Some European countries still use the name *wolfram*, although tungsten is now more widely accepted.

Where tungsten is found

Tungsten is a scarce metal, making up just a tiny fraction—around 1.5 parts per million—of Earth's crust. This is about the same concentration as tungsten's close relatives in the periodic table, molybdenum and tin. Tungsten is never found as a metal in nature. It combines with other elements to form compounds locked away in rocks called minerals. Although there are more than twenty tungsten minerals, only two—wolframite and scheelite—are important sources of the metal.

Tungsten minerals

The black-brown mineral wolframite is the main source of tungsten. This mineral is often associated with the tin ore cassiterite. Wolframite contains varying amounts of iron tungstate ($FeWO_4$) and

This is a dark gray crystal of wolframite, the main ore from which the metal tungsten is extracted. Wolframite is often associated with deposits of cassiterite, a tin ore found in or around granitic rocks.

manganese tungstate ($MnWO_4$). A mineral with more than 80 percent iron tungstate is called ferberite. A mineral with over 80 percent manganese tungstate is called hübnerite.

The other important tungsten mineral is scheelite, which varies in color from white to green. Pure scheelite fluoresces, or glows, under ultraviolet light. This mineral consists of calcium tungstate ($CaWO_4$).

Nonrenewable resource

Geologists estimate that there are at least 3.3 million tons (3 million tonnes) of tungsten reserves in the world. However, some of these deposits will be difficult and expensive to recover. Current research suggests that these deposits will last for about one hundred years.

A prospector searches for tungsten ores in Abha, Saudi Arabia. Prospectors make a living by locating new sources of valuable minerals.

TUNGSTEN FACTS	
LEADING PRODUCERS	
In 2002, the leading tungsten producers were	
China	37,000 tons (33,560 tonnes)
Russia	3,600 tons (3,265 tonnes)
Austria	1,700 tons (1,540 tonnes)
Portugal	800 tons (725 tonnes)
North Korea	600 tons (545 tonnes)
Bolivia	390 tons (350 tonnes)
Uzbekistan	150 tons (135 tonnes)
Burma	90 tons (81 tonnes)
Thailand	50 tons (45 tonnes)
Brazil	15 tons (13.6 tonnes)
Rest of the world	190 tons (172 tonnes)

Mining tungsten ores

Beralt Tin & Wolfram's Panasqueira tungsten mine in Portugal is one of the world's largest producers of tungsten concentrates outside of China.

More than half of the world's supply of tungsten comes from mines in the Nan Ling Mountains of Jiangxi, Henan, and Quangdong provinces of China. The CanTung mine in Canada's Northwest Territories is the Western world's largest tungsten operation. Russian deposits are found around the northern Caucasus and Lake Baikal. Deposits in the United States are found in Arizona, California, Nevada, and North Carolina. Most Western mines closed in the 1980s and 1990s in response to a decrease in the price of tungsten. But many of these mines recently reopened as the price recovered, and the demand for the metal increased.

Tapping the veins

Most scheelite and wolframite deposits are found in long, narrow underground veins. This is where molten rock called magma rose up from the center of Earth, cooled, and then settled many thousands of years ago. Open-pit mining methods have been used to recover tungsten ores in Australia and Canada, but most deposits are usually mined underground.

Mining methods

The method used to extract tungsten ore from underground deposits depends on the mine, but the method chosen is generally a compromise between safety and cost. Some mines operate a room-and-pillar mining method. "Rooms" are cut in the tungsten ore, leaving a series of columns, called "pillars," to support the roof. As the mining progresses, a regular pattern of rooms and pillars forms. Other mines use the bulk mining method of "slashing out the ore." This involves drilling into the face of the tungsten deposit to carve out large chunks of the ore.

Most tungsten minerals contain less than 1.5 percent useful tungsten in the form of tungsten trioxide (WO_3). To separate the mineral crystals from the

Most tungsten ore is collected from underground deposits. Miners position huge drills on rich veins of tungsten ore (top). The ore is then collected in a process called jumbo slashing (middle). A truck unloads the ore into a crusher (bottom).

rock, crushing machines break down the ore into small chunks. The chunks are then sent to an ore-dressing plant for further processing.

Scheelite taken from the Can Tung mine in Canada. After fifteen years of inactivity, the mine reopened in 2002 in response to the demand for tungsten ores.

Recycling tungsten

Around 30 percent of the world's tungsten supply comes from scrap and waste metal. Tungsten turnings, grindings, and powder, as well as compounds such as tungsten carbide (WC), can be processed into pure metal and used again. Tungsten itself is not a major pollutant, but scrap and waste tungsten often contains other metals that may harm the environment. In addition, recycling is much cheaper than disposing the waste material.

DID YOU KNOW?

CHINESE TUNGSTEN

China contains large reserves of tungsten ore, and the world market is dominated by Chinese exports. From 1999 to 2001, the authorities in China tried to increase the metal's price by controlling the release of tungsten concentrates into the world market. The plan worked, and the price of the metal soared in the West. Although the prices decreased by August 2001, the action prompted Western governments to find new sources of tungsten concentrates. Many projects are currently underway to reopen closed mines and develop new mines in tungsten-rich areas.

Processing the ore

Tungsten minerals are processed using a chemical method similar to the one that Juan José and Fausto d'Elhuyar y de Suvisa developed over two hundred years ago. The crushed ore is cleaned and treated with alkalis to form tungsten trioxide (WO_3). The trioxide is then reduced to tungsten in a hydrogen-rich atmosphere, using carbon as the reducing agent.

Preparing the ore

Prior to chemical processing, the crushed minerals are refined using a process called gravity concentration. This separates larger chunks from the workable [...] larger chunks are returned [...] crushing. Flotation separati[on...] magnetic separation, and ro[...] all used to remove impuritie[s...] the concentration of the tungsten ore.

Chemical extraction

Unlike the method used by the d'Elhuyar y de Suvisa brothers, modern extraction involves an extra step. A complex chemical

Flotation separation is often used to concentrate tungsten ore. Crushed ore is mixed with chemicals and water in a flotation tank. Air blown through the mix carries mineral-rich bubbles to the surface of the tank so that the bubbles can be skimmed off.

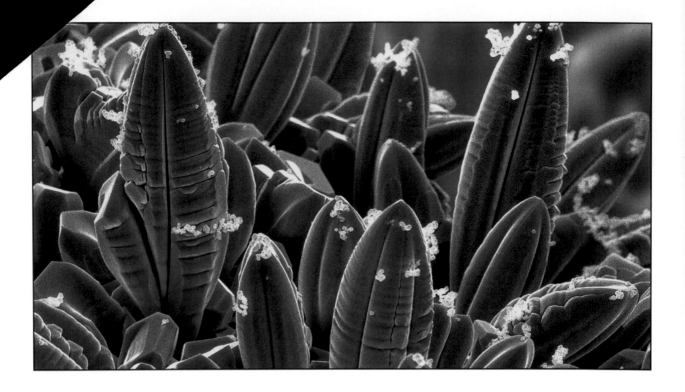

called ammonium paratungstate ($[NH_4]_{10}W_{12}O_{41}.5H_2O$), or APT for short, is produced during the reaction.

Two methods are used to produce APT: acid leaching or the autoclave-soda process. Acid leaching breaks down the ore using hydrochloric acid (HCl) to make calcium chloride ($CaCl_2$) and solid tungstic acid (H_2WO_4). The tungstic acid is dissolved in a solution of ammonia (NH_3). Crystals of APT are produced by evaporating and filtering the mixture.

In the autoclave-soda process, the ore is mixed with sodium carbonate (Na_2CO_3) at high temperature and pressure. Sodium tungstate solution ($Na_2WO_4.2H_2O$) forms, and ammonia is added. When the solution evaporates, APT crystals are left behind.

Crystals of tungsten trioxide (WO_3) are shown in this scanning electron micrograph. In the final stages of ore processing, tungsten trioxide reacts with hydrogen to produce metallic tungsten.

Producing tungsten powder

The next stage in tungsten refining is to make tungsten oxide. Tungsten forms three main oxides: tungsten trioxide (WO_3), which is yellow; a complex blue oxide ($W_{20}O_{58}$); and brown tungsten dioxide (WO_2). All three can be reduced to tungsten metal, but the blue one is the most useful in industry.

To produce the blue oxide, the APT crystals are heated in a rotary furnace. Hydrogen gas is blown over the crystals. The furnace is divided into three main temperature zones: 1,550 °F (850 °C), 1,600 °F (875 °C), and 1,650 °F (900 °C). The furnace rotates and APT crystals pass through each zone. In the hottest zone, hydrogen converts ammonia in the APT to nitrogen and hydrogen. The cooler zones stabilize the oxide as it forms. Tungsten powder is then produced by reducing the oxide with hydrogen gas in a furnace ranging from 1,025 to 1,550 °F (550 to 850 °C).

APT may also be reduced directly to the metal by a reaction with carbon at a temperature above 1,925 °F (1,050 °C). Between 1,650 and 1,925 °F (900 and 1,050 °C), the brown oxide forms. Below these temperatures, the blue oxide forms.

A sintering furnace (right) used to sinter tungsten. The "chandelier" containing the heating elements (above) is made of strips of molybdenum held in a tungsten frame.

DID YOU KNOW?

SINTERING

Tungsten powder can be packed into solid metal using a process called sintering. First, a press tightly packs the powder into bars or small ingots called billets. The bars are then heated in a furnace at 2,200 °F (1,200 °C). The bars are ready for sintering. Depending on the size of the bars, one of two methods is used. A direct sintering process is used for smaller bars. This involves passing an electric current directly through each bar. As the current increases, the bars heat up to 5,600 °F (3,100 °C), shrinking into solid metal as the powder compacts.

An indirect method is used to compact large billets. In this process, the billets are placed in a sintering furnace, which slowly heats up to 4,350 °F (2,400 °C). The billets are kept at this constant temperature for 10 hours. The process is carefully monitored to insure the billets do not crack.

Tungsten's uses and compounds

The first major use for tungsten came at the start of the twentieth century, more than two hundred years after the metal was first discovered. Electric lamp manufacturers were looking for a strong, heat-resistant material to replace the fragile carbon filaments used in most lamps. Scientists knew that tungsten was strong and had the highest melting point of all the metals. But these characteristics also made tungsten difficult to work into the fine wire needed for use as a filament.

Major breakthrough

The breakthrough came in 1903, when U.S. chemist William D. Coolidge (1873–1975) found a way of making a tungsten wire. Coolidge prepared the fine, flexible wire by tightly packing tungsten powder into thin bars and sintering them at very high temperatures. He then shaped the bars into rods from which the fine wire could be drawn. Minor improvements have been made to Coolidge's method, such as doping (adding small amounts of other substances) the filament to strengthen it and increase its resistance to melting. But the process remains much the same as the one Coolidge devised over one hundred years ago.

A tungsten filament and support is sealed into a glass bulb on a light-bulb assembly line.

Lamps and heating elements

Today, tungsten filaments are used in a wide range of lamps, from household light bulbs and automobile lamps to floodlights and reflector lamps. Tungsten filaments also have a wide range of speciality applications, such as airport runway markers and fiber-optic systems.

Tungsten filaments are also used as the heating elements for electrical furnaces. The tungsten can withstand very high temperatures for long periods. In addition, sheets of tungsten are sometimes used as heat shielding in furnaces to protect fragile parts of the furnace.

Tungsten in electronics

Tungsten filaments have important uses in the electronics industry. Very thin tungsten filaments are used almost exclusively as the material for electron emitters. These devices are used in high-intensity lamps, microwave ovens, X-ray tubes, and the cathode ray tubes (CRTs) in computer monitors and television sets. The tungsten filament forms a terminal called a cathode (a negatively charged electrode—like the negative terminal of a battery in an electric circuit). As an electric current passes through the cathode, the tungsten filament heats up and emits a narrow stream of electrons. These electrons are then used to generate microwaves to heat food in a microwave oven or to produce the image on your television set or computer monitor.

Tungsten is an ideal material for use as the heating element for a high-temperature electric furnace.

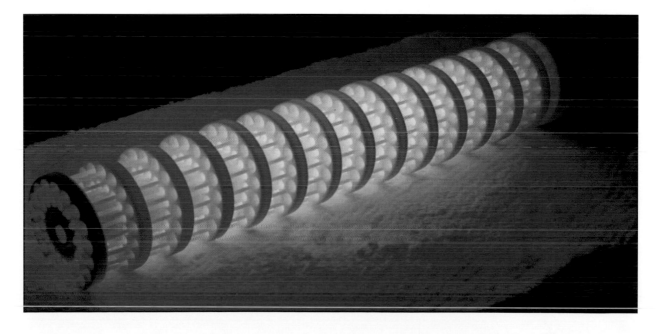

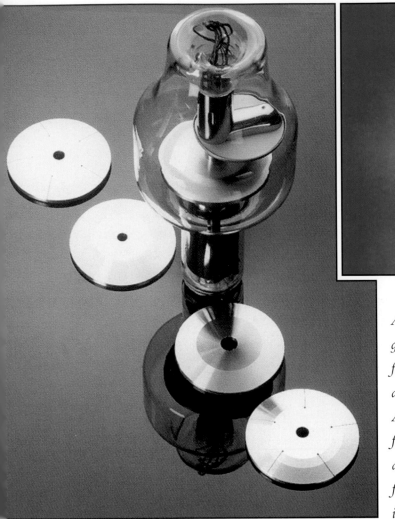

An X-ray machine consists of two electrodes inside a glass vacuum tube (left). A tungsten heating element forms the cathode. The positive terminal, or anode, is a flat tungsten disk (shown beside the vacuum tube). As an electric current heats the filament (above), the filament emits electrons. The anode draws the electrons across the tube. When an electron hits the anode, the force of the collision is so strong that a tungsten atom in the anode gives off energy in the form of an X-ray.

Tungsten wire is also used to make parts of thermometers called thermocouples. A thermocouple consists of two wires of different metals welded together at their ends. Electricity flows through the wires when the two ends are held at different temperatures. The amount of electricity that flows through the wires is a measurement of the temperature difference between the ends. If tungsten is used as one wire, the thermocouple can be used to measure very high temperatures. Tungsten is also used to make electrical contacts for use at high temperatures. This is ideal for electric arc furnaces or welding equipment, when conventional contact materials, such as copper and silver, would melt.

Chemical applications

Tungsten is relatively inert, which means that it does not readily react with many other substances. Some compounds can be made in the laboratory. Tungsten carbide (WC) is the most important artificial compound. It has a wide range of uses in industry. Tungsten and its compounds are also useful catalysts that speed up certain chemical reactions.

Many other industries rely on tungsten and its compounds. Tungsten disulfide was first developed as a lubricant for the Mariner deep space probes launched by the National Aeronautics and Space Administration (NASA). Lubricants reduce the friction between rubbing surfaces. Tungsten disulfide works well as a lubricant at high temperatures. It is now used in the plastics industry.

Some tungsten compounds are used as pigments—chemicals that add color to things. Tungstic acid and tungsten oxide form bright yellow pigments for ceramic glazes and enamels. Barium tungstate ($BaWO_4$) and zinc tungstate ($ZnWO_4$) form white pigments. A complex tungsten compound called phosphotungstic acid also helps to make bright pigments. The phosphotungstic acid reacts with organic (carbon-containing) dyes to form brilliant blue to green pigments.

Other uses

Tungsten has many other applications. Mixed with plastic, for example, tungsten's high density makes it useful as a weight on fishing rods. Another unusual use for tungsten oxide is in the manufacture of self-darkening window panes that are clear at night or in poor light but darken in bright sunshine.

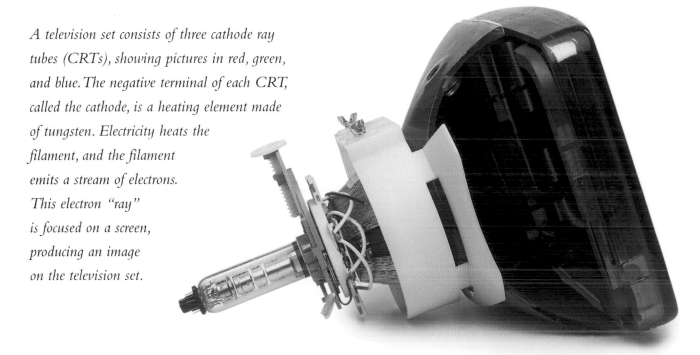

A television set consists of three cathode ray tubes (CRTs), showing pictures in red, green, and blue. The negative terminal of each CRT, called the cathode, is a heating element made of tungsten. Electricity heats the filament, and the filament emits a stream of electrons. This electron "ray" is focused on a screen, producing an image on the television set.

Tungsten alloys

Tungsten can be mixed with many other elements to make substances called alloys. Most alloys consist of metals mixed with other metals or elements such as carbon. Each element added contributes unique characteristics to the alloy, such as increased strength or resistance to wear or corrosion. One of the most important tungsten alloys is tungsten steel. It is extremely strong, hard-wearing, and stable at high temperatures.

Developing tungsten steel

In 1857, Dr. Robert Oxland patented a process to make tungsten steel. Initially, steel manufacturers could not afford to use tungsten in a large-scale industrial process. By the end of the nineteenth century, however, tungsten was much less expensive. Tungsten quickly gained popularity as an alloying agent in the steel industry. Tungsten steel finally hit the headlines in 1900 at the Exposition Universelle (World Exhibition) in Paris, when the American Bethlehem Steel Company exhibited a range of tool steels.

Tool steels

As their name suggests, tool steels are used to make tools for working, cutting, and forming materials such as metals,

The space shuttle Atlantis *launched from Cape Canaveral on August 2, 1991. Tungsten-steel alloys are widely used to make rocket-engine nozzles and other parts that operate at very high temperatures.*

plastics, and wood. As a result, tool steels must be strong and tough over a wide range of temperatures.

There are many different kinds of tool steels. High-speed steels (HSS) contain at least 7 percent tungsten, molybdenum, and vanadium, with smaller amounts of carbon. The term *high-speed* refers to the speed at which the tools can cut metals. HSS are used to make a wide range of cutting tools, from drills and gear cutters to lathe tools and saw blades. Tools made from HSS are often coated with a thin layer of titanium nitride (TiN), which makes the tools last longer as well as increasing their cutting speed.

Shock-resistant tool steels are among the toughest of all the HSS. They are used to make screwdrivers, chisels, and riveting

A wind tunnel test on a model of a space shuttle simulates the conditions a shuttle faces when reentering Earth's atmosphere. Materials such as ceramic tiles and tungsten alloys form a heat-resistant shield to protect the space shuttle during reentry.

tools. Shock-resistant tool steels are also called cold-work tool steels. These tools are designed for use at low temperatures. Tools used at temperatures of 930 °F (500 °C) or higher are made from hot-work tool steels. Water-hardening tool steels have high resistance to surface wear, but they do not stay as hard at high temperatures. Typical applications for water-hardening tool steels include drills and files.

DID YOU KNOW?

TUNGSTEN SHORTAGE

Tungsten was an extremely valuable commodity during World War II (1939–1945). Tungsten-steel alloys were needed for tools to make vehicles, weapons, and other military equipment. But a tungsten shortage forced steel manufacturers in Europe and the United States to look for a replacement. They chose molybdenum—another metallic element with similar characteristics to tungsten. Molybdenum proved to be an excellent substitute. Not only was it cheaper than tungsten, but less molybdenum was needed to make an alloy with similar properties to tungsten steel.

Heat-resisting steels

Tungsten is added to corrosion-resistant steels that need to operate over higher temperature ranges. Heat-resisting steels are chromium-nickel steel alloys, with a maximum of 6 percent tungsten. Heat-resisting steels are used to make gas turbines, oil-cracking units, furnace conveyor belts, and the valves for automobile combustion engines. The alloys combine hardness and corrosion resistance at high temperatures.

Many darts are made from tungsten alloyed with iron and copper or nickel. Tungsten's high density allows for a slimmer dart that retains its weight. A slimmer dart also makes it easier for the player to group the darts closer on the dartboard.

A range of small-caliber bullets made with a composite of tungsten, tin, and zinc. The U.S. military hopes to replace all lead-based ammunition by the year 2005.

Other tungsten alloys

Tungsten forms different alloys with many other elements. Stellite is the tradename given to a series of alloys containing cobalt, chromium, and tungsten combined with a range of other elements. Stellites are used to make bearings, pistons, and many other products in which durability and resistance to wear is required.

As its name suggests, tungsten heavy metal, or Heavimet for short, is a heavy tungsten-bearing material. Heavimet consists of tungsten powder bound with an alloy of iron and nickel or copper. It is made by sintering the tungsten–alloy mixture. The alloy melts and binds the tungsten particles in a strong cement. Heavimet is used to make armor-piercing ammunition, dart barrels, and the weights for golf clubheads.

DID YOU KNOW?

GREEN BULLETS

Every year, soldiers in the U.S. Army fire an estimated two hundred million rounds of small caliber ammunition during military training exercises. But the lead in these bullets poses a huge threat to the environment. It poisons wildlife and enters domestic water supplies. In response, the U.S. military has developed lead-free bullets, dubbed "green bullets." These are made of a tungsten-tin-zinc composite. The green bullets are just as effective as traditional ammunition but pose far less of an environmental threat.

Superalloys are extremely strong alloys consisting of cobalt, iron, or nickel mixed with a high content of tungsten, tantalum, molybdenum, and rhenium. Turbine blades for airplanes and spacecraft are made from superalloys. The alloys combine high mechanical strength with erosion resistance at very high temperatures.

Tungsten alloys are also important in the electronics industry. Some alloys replace tungsten metal for use in electrical contacts or filaments. Tungsten–copper alloys are also used as heat sinks for computer microprocessors. Processors generate as much heat as a household cooker—the heat sink removes this heat.

Tungsten carbide

Tungsten carbide is a hard compound with a gray, metallic appearance. There are two forms of tungsten carbide: WC or W_2C. In these forms either one or two tungsten atoms are bonded to a carbon atom. The WC form is the most important in industry. It can be used alone, or in combination with other metals, to make drill bit tips, the cutting edges of tools, and armor-piercing ammunition.

The blade of this electric planer is made from ultrasharp tungsten carbide.

Making tungsten carbide

Tungsten carbide is manufactured by heating tungsten powder with carbon in a stream of hydrogen gas. The furnace must be kept at a temperature between 2,550 and 2,900 °F (1,400 and 1,600 °C).

Cemented carbides

In the 1920s, a German company called Osram succeeded in combining tungsten carbide and cobalt using a process called liquid phase sintering. First, they molded the cobalt powder and grains of tungsten into the right shape. During the sintering process, the heat melted the cobalt powder and bound the tungsten carbide grains in

a strong cement. This process resulted in a very hard substance called cemented carbide, or hardmetal. Modern hardmetal production has largely stayed the same. However, improvements in sintering technology and tungsten carbide production has led to higher standards in hardmetal quality.

Cemented carbides are now the industry standard for mining tools and other wear-resistant machinery. Today, mining tools are coated with alternate layers of alumina (aluminum oxide; Al_2O_3), titanium nitride, and other hard materials to prolong their lifetimes. Another development is the range of tungsten carbide grain sizes in cemented carbides. Chemists have found that the hardmetal's hardness and resistance to wear increase as the grain size decreases.

This picture shows one of the tunnel-boring machines (TBMs) used to dig the Channel Tunnel, which links Britain with mainland Europe. The cutting face of the TBM is made from cemented carbide.

DID YOU KNOW?

MOHS' HARDNESS SCALE

German mineralogist Friedrich Mohs (1773–1839) developed a scale to measure the hardness of different materials in 1812. Mohs' scale has ten separate divisions, although they are not divided in equal intervals. Mohs gave a value of 10 to the hardness of diamond, which is the hardest natural mineral. He gave a value of 1 to talc— one of the softest minerals in nature. Tungsten carbide is noted for its hardness. It has a value of 9.5 on Mohs' hardness scale.

Periodic table

Everything in the universe consists of combinations of substances called elements. Elements consist of tiny atoms, which are too small to see. Atoms are the building blocks of matter.

The character of an atom depends on how many even tinier particles called protons are in its center, or nucleus. An element's atomic number is the same as the number of its protons.

Scientists have found around 110 different elements. About 90 elements occur naturally on Earth. The rest have been made in laboratories.

All the chemical elements are set out on a chart called the periodic table. This lists all the elements in order according to their atomic number.

The elements at the left of the table are metals. Those at the right are nonmetals. Between the metals and the nonmetals are the metalloids, which sometimes act like metals and sometimes like nonmetals.

● On the left of the table are the alkali metals. These elements have just one electron in their outer shells.

● Elements get more reactive as you go down a group.

● On the right of the periodic table are the noble gases. These elements have full outer shells.

● The number of electrons orbiting the nucleus increases down each group.

● Elements in the same group have the same number of electrons in their outer shells.

● The transition metals are in the middle of the table, between Groups II and III.

Group I

Group II

Transition metals

Group I	Group II							
1 H Hydrogen 1								
3 Li Lithium 7	4 Be Beryllium 9							
11 Na Sodium 23	12 Mg Magnesium 24							
19 K Potassium 39	20 Ca Calcium 40	21 Sc Scandium 45	22 Ti Titanium 48	23 V Vanadium 51	24 Cr Chromium 52	25 Mn Manganese 55	26 Fe Iron 56	27 Co Cobalt 59
37 Rb Rubidium 85	38 Sr Strontium 88	39 Y Yttrium 89	40 Zr Zirconium 91	41 Nb Niobium 93	42 Mo Molybdenum 96	43 Tc Technetium (98)	44 Ru Ruthenium 101	45 Rh Rhodium 103
55 Cs Cesium 133	56 Ba Barium 137	71 Lu Lutetium 175	72 Hf Hafnium 179	73 Ta Tantalum 181	74 W Tungsten 184	75 Re Rhenium 186	76 Os Osmium 190	77 Ir Iridium 192
87 Fr Francium 223	88 Ra Radium 226	103 Lr Lawrencium (260)	104 Unq Unnilquadium (261)	105 Unp Unnilpentium (262)	106 Unh Unnilhexium (263)	107 Uns Unnilseptium (?)	108 Uno Unniloctium (?)	109 Une Unilenium (?)

Lanthanide elements

Actinide elements

57 La Lanthanum 139	58 Ce Cerium 140	59 Pr Praseodymium 141	60 Nd Neodymium 144	61 Pm Promethium (145)
89 Ac Actinium 227	90 Th Thorium 232	91 Pa Protactinium 231	92 U Uranium 238	93 Np Neptunium (237)

The horizontal rows of the table are called periods. As you go across a period, the atomic number increases by one from each element to the next. The vertical columns are called groups. Elements get heavier as you go down a group. All the elements in a group have the same number of electrons in their outer shells. This means they react in similar ways.

The transition metals fall between Groups II and III. Their electron shells fill up in an unusual way. The lanthanide elements and the actinide elements are set apart from the main table to make it easier to read. All the lanthanide elements and the actinide elements are quite rare.

Tungsten in the table

Tungsten is one of the transition metals that form a block in the middle of the periodic table. The chemistry of transition metals is rather unusual. In most elements, only electrons in the outer electron shell are involved in chemical reactions. In the transition metals, electrons in the last two electron shells are involved.

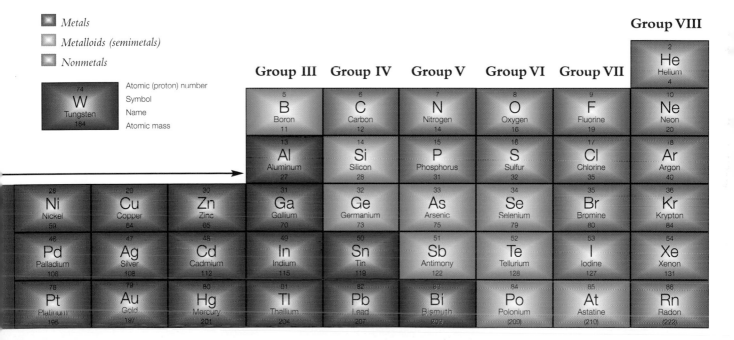

Chemical reactions

Chemical reactions are going on all the time—candles burn, nails rust, and food is digested. Some reactions involve just two substances, others many more. But whenever a reaction takes place, at least one substance is changed.

In a chemical reaction, the atoms do not change. A hydrogen atom remains a hydrogen atom; a tungsten atom remains a tungsten atom. But they join together in new combinations to form new molecules.

Writing an equation

Chemical reactions can be described by writing down the atoms and molecules before and after the reaction. Since the atoms stay the same, the number of atoms before will be the same as the number of atoms after. Chemists write the reaction as

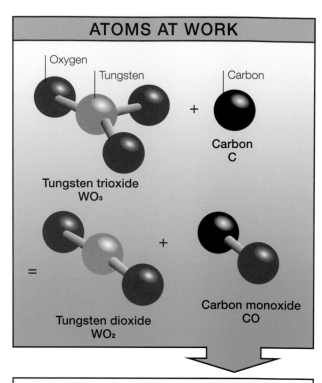

ATOMS AT WORK

Oxygen

Tungsten

Carbon

Tungsten trioxide
WO_3

+

Carbon
C

=

+

Tungsten dioxide
WO_2

Carbon monoxide
CO

The reaction that takes place when tungsten trioxide is reduced by carbon can be written like this:

$$WO_3 + C \rightarrow WO_2 + CO$$

a chemical equation. Equations are a quick and easy way of showing what happens during a chemical reaction.

Making it balance

When the numbers of each atom on both sides of the equation are equal, the equation is balanced. If the numbers are not equal, the chemist adjusts the number of atoms until the equation balances.

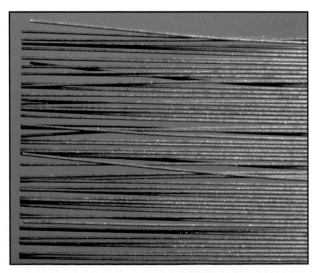

NASA has developed a temperature-resistant tape for use in gas turbine engines. The tape is made from the metal niobium reinforced with tungsten fibers.

30

Glossary

alloy: A mixture of a metal with another element, often another metal.

atom: The smallest part of an element having all the properties of that element. Each atom is less than a millionth of an inch in diameter.

atomic mass: The number of protons and neutrons in an atom.

atomic number: The number of protons in an atom.

bond: The attraction between two atoms or ions that holds them together.

catalyst: Something that makes a chemical reaction occur more quickly.

compound: A substance made of atoms of more than one element. The atoms are held together by chemical bonds.

crystal: A solid substance in which the atoms are arranged in a regular, three-dimensional pattern.

electrode: A material through which an electrical current flows into, or out of, a liquid electrolyte.

electrolyte: A liquid that electricity can flow through.

electron: A tiny particle with a negative charge. Electrons are found inside atoms, where they move around the nucleus in layers called electron shells.

element: A substance that is made from only one type of atom.

ion: A particle of an element similar to an atom but carrying an additional negative or positive electrical charge.

isotopes: Atoms of an element with the same number of protons and electrons but different number of neutrons.

metal: An element on the left-hand side of the periodic table.

mineral: A compound or element as it is found in its natural form on Earth.

molecule: A particle that contains atoms held together by chemical bonds.

neutron: A tiny particle with no electrical charge. Neutrons are found in the nucleus of almost every atom.

nucleus: The dense structure at the center of an atom.

ores: Rocks that contain natural forms of compounds or elements.

periodic table: A chart containing all the chemical elements laid out in order of their atomic number.

proton: A tiny particle with a positive charge. Protons are found inside the nucleus of an atom.

radioactivity: The release of energy caused by particle changes in the nucleus.

reduction: A reaction in which a substance loses oxygen atoms or electrons.

refining: An industrial process that frees substances, such as metals, from impurities or unwanted material.

sintering: Using heat or electricity to compact powdery substances into solids.

Index